K. CONNORS

Python Programming for Kids

A Fun and Easy Guide to Learning Coding, Building Games, and Creating Projects

Copyright © 2024 by K. Connors

All rights reserved. No part of this publication may be reproduced, stored or transmitted in any form or by any means, electronic, mechanical, photocopying, recording, scanning, or otherwise without written permission from the publisher. It is illegal to copy this book, post it to a website, or distribute it by any other means without permission.

First edition

This book was professionally typeset on Reedsy.
Find out more at reedsy.com

Contents

Introduction	1
Chapter 1: Getting Started with Python	6
Chapter 2: Basic Python Concepts	11
Chapter 3: Control Structures	17
Chapter 4: Functions and Modules	24
Chapter 5: Working with Lists and Dictionaries	30
Chapter 6: Introduction to Object-Oriented Programming	34
Chapter 7: Working with Files	40
Chapter 8: Fun with Turtle Graphics	47
Chapter 9: Simple Game Development	51
Chapter 10: Building Your First Project	58
Conclusion	62

Introduction

Hey there, young programmer! Are you ready to dive into the world of Python programming? Don't worry if you've never heard of Python before, or if the idea of programming sounds a bit intimidating. By the time you finish this book, you'll be a budding programmer, creating fun projects and amazing programs.

Let's start with the basics. What is Python, and why should you care about it? Well, Python is a type of language, but not the kind you speak. It's a language for computers. Think of it as a way to talk to your computer and tell it what to do. And the best part? It's one of the easiest computer languages to learn. Even big companies like Google, NASA, and Disney use Python to create all sorts of cool stuff.

Now, you might wonder why it's called Python. Does it have anything to do with snakes? Not really. Python got its name from a British comedy show called "Monty Python's Flying Circus." The creators of Python wanted the language to be fun and not too serious, which makes it perfect for kids like you to learn.

Before we start writing any code, let's set the stage. First, you need to install Python on your computer. Don't worry, it's simpler than it sounds. Head over to the Python website and download the latest version. Follow the instructions, and you'll have Python ready to go in no time. Once it's installed, you'll need a place to write your code. This place is called an Integrated Development Environment, or IDE for short. An IDE is like a supercharged notebook where you can write, test, and run your programs. A great IDE for beginners is called IDLE, and it comes with Python. So, you're all set to begin.

Let's talk a bit about why learning to code is awesome. Imagine being able to create your own games, solve puzzles, or even build tools to help you with your homework. Programming teaches you how to think logically and solve problems step-by-step, which is a superpower you can use in all sorts of areas, not just with computers. Plus, it's a lot of fun! You get to create something out of nothing, just by typing on your keyboard.

When you start learning Python, you'll notice that it looks a bit like English. That's one of the reasons it's so great for beginners. The commands and structures are straightforward and easy to understand. For example, if you want your program to print something on the screen, you just use the word "print." Simple, right?

As we go through this book, we'll break everything down into small, easy-to-understand pieces. Each chapter will build on what you've learned before, so by the end, you'll have a strong foundation in Python programming. We'll start with the basics, like what variables are and how to use them. Then we'll move on to more exciting stuff, like making decisions in your programs and repeating actions with loops.

But enough about that for now. Let's talk about what you'll need to get started. Besides your computer and Python, you'll need a good attitude and a bit of patience. Sometimes, programming can be tricky, and things might not work the way you expect them to. That's okay. Every programmer, no matter how experienced, runs into bugs and errors. The important thing is to keep trying and not get discouraged. Remember, every mistake is a chance to learn something new.

INTRODUCTION

One of the cool things about programming is that you don't have to do it alone. There's a whole community of programmers out there who are ready to help. If you get stuck, you can ask for help online, watch tutorials, or even join coding clubs and meetups. Learning to code is a journey, and it's more fun when you share it with others.

Let's take a moment to talk about what you can expect as you learn to code. At first, things might seem a bit strange or confusing. You'll learn new terms like "syntax" and "loops," and it might feel like you're learning a new language. But don't worry. Just like learning to ride a bike or play a new game, the more you practice, the better you'll get. And soon, things that seemed hard at first will start to make sense.

As we move through each chapter, we'll include little exercises and projects for you to try. These will help you practice what you've learned and see how it all fits together. By the time you reach the end of the book, you'll have created your own programs and maybe even your own little games. How cool is that?

Now, you might be wondering, "Why Python? Why not another programming language?" Well, Python is special because it's both powerful and easy to learn. It's used in many different fields, from web development to scientific research, and even in creating video games. Python is like a Swiss Army knife for programmers. It has tools for just about everything, and it's designed to be friendly and easy to use, especially for beginners.

Okay, let's talk a bit more about what you'll actually be doing with Python. We'll start with simple things like making the computer do some math for you. You'll learn how to create and use variables, which are like little containers that hold information. Then, we'll move on to making decisions in your code. This means you can tell the computer to do something different depending on the situation, just like you make decisions every day.

After that, we'll dive into loops. Loops are super cool because they let you repeat actions over and over without having to write the same code again and again. This is great for things like counting, drawing shapes, or even making animations. Speaking of which, we'll also play around with Turtle Graphics, a fun way to create pictures and designs with code. It's like having a little robot turtle that follows your instructions to draw on the screen.

We'll also explore how to work with files. Imagine being able to save your high scores from a game you created, or read a list of your favorite books from a file. You'll learn how to open, read, and write files, which opens up a whole new world of possibilities.

As you get more comfortable with Python, we'll tackle more complex topics like functions and modules. Functions are like mini-programs within your program. They help you organize your code and make it easier to understand and reuse. Modules are collections of functions and tools that you can use in your programs. Python has a huge library of modules for all sorts of tasks, from math and science to web development and gaming.

One of the most exciting parts of this book will be learning about object-oriented programming, or OOP for short. OOP might sound complicated, but it's a powerful way to think about and organize your code. You'll learn how to create classes and objects, which are like blueprints for your programs. This will help you build more complex and interesting projects.

By the end of this book, you'll have all the tools you need to start creating your own projects. Whether you want to build a game, create art, or solve puzzles, you'll have the skills to make your ideas come to life. And who knows? Maybe you'll even inspire your friends to start coding too.

So, are you ready to embark on this adventure? Grab your computer, fire up Python, and let's get coding. Remember, learning to program is like going on a treasure hunt. There will be challenges along the way, but each step brings you closer to discovering something amazing. Let's start this journey together

INTRODUCTION

and see where your creativity and curiosity can take you.

Welcome to the world of Python programming. Let's have some fun and make something awesome!

Chapter 1: Getting Started with Python

Welcome to your first step into the world of Python programming! This is going to be a fun and exciting journey where you'll learn how to talk to your computer and make it do all sorts of cool things. Don't worry if you don't know anything about programming yet. We're starting right from the beginning, and I'll be here to guide you all the way.

First things first, let's talk about what Python is. Python is a programming language, and just like any other language, it's a way of communicating. But instead of talking to people, you're talking to your computer. You give it instructions, and it follows them. Python is known for being easy to read and write, which makes it a great choice for beginners.

Now, before we start coding, we need to set up Python on your computer. This is a bit like setting up a new game. You need to download and install it first. Head over to the official Python website. You'll see a big button that says "Download Python." Click on it and choose the version that matches your operating system, whether it's Windows, Mac, or Linux. Follow the instructions to install it. If you need help, ask an adult or check out some online tutorials.

Once you have Python installed, you'll need a place to write your code. This place is called an Integrated Development Environment, or IDE for short. Think of it as a fancy notebook for programmers. The good news is, Python comes with its own IDE called IDLE. When you open IDLE, you'll see a window that looks a bit like a blank text document. This is where you'll write your programs.

Let's start with something simple. Open IDLE and type the following line:

print("Hello, world!")

Now, press Enter. What happened? You should see the words "Hello, world!" appear on the screen. Congratulations, you just wrote your first Python program! The print function is one of the most basic and useful functions in Python. It tells the computer to display whatever is inside the parentheses.

Great, now let's learn about variables. In programming, variables are like little containers that hold information. You can store numbers, text, and other data in them. Here's how you create a variable in Python: name equals "Alice". In this example, name is the variable, and "Alice" is the information stored in it. You can choose any name you like for your variables, as long as it doesn't start with a number and doesn't include spaces.

Try typing this into IDLE: age equals 10. Now you have a variable called age that stores the number 10. You can use variables to do all sorts of things. For example, you can print them out. When you run these lines, Python will display "Alice" and 10 on the screen. You can also use variables in calculations. Let's try something fun. Type this: year equals 2023, birth_year equals year minus age, print(birth_year). Python will calculate the birth year based on the current year and your age. It's like having your own personal math assistant.

Next, let's talk about data types. In Python, data can come in different forms. The most common types are strings (text), integers (whole numbers), and floats (decimal numbers). You've already seen strings and integers. Here's how you create a float: height equals 4.5. Now you have a variable called height that stores the number 4.5. You can use these different types of data in your programs to perform various tasks.

Another important concept in programming is comments. Comments are lines in your code that Python ignores. They're useful for adding notes or explanations to your code. To write a comment, start the line with a hash symbol. Comments won't affect how your program runs, but they're very helpful for keeping track of what your code does, especially when your programs get more complex.

Let's move on to some basic math operations. Python can handle addition, subtraction, multiplication, and division. Here are some examples: sum equals 5 plus 3, difference equals 7 minus 2, product equals 4 times 3, quotient equals 8 divided by 2. When you run these lines, Python will perform the calculations and store the results in the variables sum, difference, product, and quotient. You can print these variables to see the results.

Python can also handle more advanced math operations. For example, to find the remainder of a division, use the percent symbol. remainder equals 10 percent 3. This will display 1, because 10 divided by 3 leaves a remainder of 1. Another useful operation is exponentiation, which means raising a number to a power. Use the double asterisk symbol for this: square equals 4 double asterisk 2, cube equals 2 double asterisk 3. Python will calculate 4 squared (16) and 2 cubed (8) for you. These basic math operations are very handy and will be used frequently as you learn more about programming.

Now that you know some basics, let's try a simple program that uses variables and math. We'll create a program that calculates the area of a rectangle. Here's how to do it: length equals 5, width equals 3, area equals length times width, print("The area of the rectangle is:", area). When you run this program, Python will multiply the length and width to find the area, and then print the result. This is a great example of how you can use programming to solve real-world problems.

One of the powerful features of Python is its ability to make decisions using if statements. An if statement tells the computer to do something only if a certain condition is true. Here's an example: number equals 7, if number is greater than 5 then print("The number is greater than 5"). In this example, Python checks if the number is greater than 5. If it is, it prints a message. You can also add an else clause to handle the opposite case. Now Python will print one message if the condition is true and another message if it's false. You can also chain multiple conditions together using elif, which stands for "else if." This way, Python will check each condition in order until it finds one that's true. This allows you to create more complex decision-making in your programs.

Another useful feature in Python is loops. Loops let you repeat actions multiple times without having to write the same code over and over. There are two main types of loops in Python: for loops and while loops. A for loop repeats a block of code a certain number of times. The range function generates a sequence of numbers, and the for loop iterates over that sequence, printing each number. You can use for loops to do all sorts of things, like counting, creating patterns, or processing items in a list.

A while loop repeats a block of code as long as a certain condition is true. Here's an example that prints the numbers from 1 to 5 using a while loop: i equals 1, while i is less than or equal to 5 then print(i), increment i by 1. In this example, the while loop continues to run as long as the variable i is less than or equal to 5. The line increment i by 1 increases the value of i by 1 each time the loop runs, which eventually makes the condition false and stops the loop.

Loops are incredibly powerful and allow you to automate repetitive tasks. You'll find them very useful as you start writing more complex programs.

By now, you've learned quite a few fundamental concepts in Python. You know how to use variables, perform basic math operations, make decisions with if statements, and repeat actions with loops. These are the building blocks of programming, and you'll use them in almost every program you write.

As we move forward, we'll build on these basics and explore more advanced topics. But for now, take some time to practice what you've learned. Try writing your own programs, experimenting with different variables, and using loops and if statements to create interesting patterns and solve problems.

Remember, programming is a skill that gets better with practice. The more you code, the more comfortable you'll become. And don't worry if you make mistakes along the way. Every programmer does. What's important is to keep trying and learning from those mistakes. With Python, you have a powerful tool at your fingertips. You can create games, solve puzzles, automate tasks, and so much more. So keep coding, keep experimenting, and most importantly, have fun.

Chapter 2: Basic Python Concepts

Welcome back, young programmer! Now that you've dipped your toes into the world of Python with some basic commands, it's time to dive a bit deeper. In this chapter, we're going to explore some fundamental concepts that are crucial for every programmer to understand. Don't worry, we'll take it step by step, and before you know it, you'll be coding like a pro.

Let's start with a deeper look at variables. You already know that variables are like little containers that hold information. But did you know that there are different types of variables? Python is a bit like a super-organized closet, where every item has its own specific place. Variables in Python can store different types of data, such as numbers, text, or even lists of items.

We've talked about strings, integers, and floats. Strings are sequences of characters, like words or sentences. They are always enclosed in quotes, either single or double. For example, "Hello, world!" is a string. Strings can be quite powerful. You can join them together, split them apart, or even find and replace characters within them. This is called string manipulation.

Integers, on the other hand, are whole numbers. They don't have any decimal points. So, numbers like 3, 42, and 1000 are all integers. When you do math with integers, you're performing basic arithmetic operations that you learned in school. Python makes it easy to add, subtract, multiply, and divide integers.

Floats are numbers that have a decimal point. They're useful for more precise calculations. For example, the number 3.14 is a float. Floats are handled a bit differently by computers than integers because they need to keep track of the position of the decimal point. This can sometimes lead to small rounding errors in your calculations, but don't worry too much about that for now.

Let's talk about some basic operations you can perform with these data types. For instance, you can combine strings using the plus symbol. If you have two strings, "Hello" and "world", you can join them together like this: "Hello" + "world". This is called string concatenation. The result would be "Helloworld". If you want a space between the words, you just add it in: "Hello" + " " + "world" which gives you "Hello world".

For numbers, Python supports all the usual arithmetic operations. You can add, subtract, multiply, and divide numbers just like you would on a calculator. There are also some special operations you might find useful. For example, the double asterisk symbol is used for exponentiation, which means raising a number to a power. So, 2 ** 3 is 2 raised to the power of 3, which equals 8.

Now, let's move on to something called lists. A list is a collection of items. You can think of it as a shopping list or a to-do list. Lists are very powerful in Python because they let you store multiple pieces of data in one place. You create a list by placing items inside square brackets, separated by commas. For example, [1, 2, 3, 4, 5] is a list of numbers. Lists can also hold strings, or even a mix of different data types.

Lists have many useful features. You can add items to a list, remove items, or even sort the list in different ways. One of the most useful things about lists is that you can access individual items by their position, called an index. In Python, lists are zero-indexed, which means the first item is at position 0, the second item is at position 1, and so on. So, if you have a list called numbers and you want to get the first item, you would write numbers[0].

CHAPTER 2: BASIC PYTHON CONCEPTS

Python also allows you to slice lists, which means you can take a portion of a list. For example, if you have a list of numbers from 0 to 9, you can get the first three numbers by writing numbers[0:3]. This gives you a new list with the first three items.

Another powerful feature in Python is the dictionary. A dictionary is a collection of key-value pairs. You can think of it like a real dictionary, where each word (the key) has a definition (the value). In Python, you create a dictionary by placing items inside curly braces, with each key and value separated by a colon. For example, {"name": "Alice", "age": 10} is a dictionary with two key-value pairs. You can access the value for a specific key by writing the key in square brackets, like this: person["name"].

Dictionaries are very flexible and can hold different types of data. You can add new key-value pairs, remove them, or even change the values. This makes dictionaries very useful for storing and organizing data.

Next, let's talk about functions. Functions are blocks of code that perform a specific task. You've already seen the print function, which displays text on the screen. Python has many built-in functions, but you can also create your own. To define a function, you use the def keyword, followed by the function name and parentheses. Inside the parentheses, you can list any parameters the function needs. Parameters are like variables that you pass into the function. Here's a simple example of a function that adds two numbers:

```
def add_numbers(a, b):
    return a + b
```

In this example, add_numbers is the name of the function, and a and b are the parameters. The function adds the two numbers and returns the result. To use the function, you call it by its name and pass in the arguments, like this: add_numbers(3, 5). The function will return 8.

Functions are very useful because they let you reuse code. If you find yourself writing the same code over and over, you can put it in a function and call the function whenever you need it. This makes your code more organized and easier to read.

Another important concept in Python is loops. Loops let you repeat a block of code multiple times. There are two main types of loops in Python: for loops and while loops. A for loop repeats a block of code for each item in a sequence, such as a list. Here's an example of a for loop that prints each item in a list:

```
numbers = [1, 2, 3, 4, 5]
    for number in numbers:
    print(number)
```

In this example, the for loop iterates over each item in the list and prints it. Loops are very powerful because they let you automate repetitive tasks.

A while loop repeats a block of code as long as a certain condition is true. Here's an example of a while loop that prints numbers from 1 to 5:

```
i = 1
    while i <= 5:
    print(i)
    i += 1
```

In this example, the while loop continues to run as long as the variable i is less than or equal to 5. The line i += 1 increases the value of i by 1 each time the loop runs, which eventually makes the condition false and stops the loop.

Loops are incredibly useful in programming. They let you perform repetitive tasks without having to write the same code over and over. As you start writing more complex programs, you'll find yourself using loops a lot.

CHAPTER 2: BASIC PYTHON CONCEPTS

Another important topic we need to cover is control flow. Control flow is the order in which your code is executed. Python executes your code line by line, from top to bottom. However, you can change the control flow using if statements, loops, and functions.

If statements let you make decisions in your code. You've already seen a simple if statement that checks if a number is greater than 5. You can also use if statements to compare strings, check if an item is in a list, or even combine multiple conditions. If statements are very powerful and allow you to create complex logic in your programs.

Let's talk about another important concept: input and output. So far, we've only been printing text to the screen. But what if you want to get input from the user? Python makes this easy with the input function. The input function displays a prompt and waits for the user to type something. Here's an example:

```
name = input("What is your name? ")
    print("Hello, " + name + "!")
```

In this example, the input function displays the prompt "What is your name?" and waits for the user to type their name. The user's input is then stored in the variable name, and the program prints a personalized greeting. Input and output are very important in programming because they let your programs interact with the user.

Finally, let's talk about error handling. No matter how careful you are, you're going to run into errors in your code. Python has a way to handle these errors gracefully using try and except blocks. Here's an example:

```
try:
    result = 10 / 0
    except ZeroDivisionError:
    print("You can't divide by zero!")
```

In this example, the try block contains code that might raise an error. If an error occurs, the code in the except block is executed. This allows you to handle errors and keep your program running smoothly. Error handling is very important because it makes your programs more robust and user-friendly.

We've covered a lot of ground in this chapter. You've learned about variables, data types, lists, dictionaries, functions, loops, control flow, input and output, and error handling. These are the basic building blocks of programming, and you'll use them in almost every program you write.

As you continue your journey into Python programming, remember to practice what you've learned. The more you code, the more comfortable you'll become. And don't be afraid to experiment and try new things. Programming is a skill that gets better with practice, and every mistake is a chance to learn something new. Keep coding, and have fun exploring the amazing world of Python.

Chapter 3: Control Structures

Python programming becomes even more exciting when you can control the flow of your code. Control structures are the tools that allow you to decide what your program should do and when it should do it. This chapter will cover if statements, for loops, and while loops, which are the main building blocks for controlling your program's flow.

An if statement is like asking a question and doing something based on the answer. It checks a condition and executes a block of code if the condition is true. If the condition is not true, you can tell it to do something else with an else clause. Here's a simple example:

```
if number > 5:
    print("The number is greater than 5")
else:
    print("The number is 5 or less")
```

In this example, if the variable number is greater than 5, Python prints "The number is greater than 5." If the number is not greater than 5, Python prints "The number is 5 or less." The else part is optional, so you can leave it out if you only want to do something when the condition is true.

Sometimes, you need to check multiple conditions. That's where elif comes in, which stands for "else if." Here's an example with elif:

```
if number > 5:
    print("The number is greater than 5")
elif number == 5:
    print("The number is exactly 5")
else:
    print("The number is less than 5")
```

Now, Python checks if the number is greater than 5 first. If it is, it prints the first message. If not, it checks if the number is exactly 5 and prints the second message. If neither condition is true, it prints the third message. This allows you to handle multiple scenarios in your code.

Next, let's talk about loops. Loops let you repeat a block of code multiple times. There are two main types of loops in Python: for loops and while loops.

A for loop is great when you know how many times you want to repeat something. It's like counting the number of laps in a race. Here's a basic for loop:

```
for i in range(5):
    print(i)
```

The range function generates a sequence of numbers from 0 to 4. The for loop goes through each number in the sequence and prints it. So, this loop prints the numbers 0, 1, 2, 3, and 4. You can also use a for loop to go through items in a list:

```
fruits = ["apple", "banana", "cherry"]
    for fruit in fruits:
    print(fruit)
```

In this example, the for loop goes through each item in the list fruits and prints it. Loops are very powerful and can save you a lot of time by automating repetitive tasks.

A while loop is used when you want to keep doing something as long as a certain condition is true. It's like keeping your eyes open while you're watching for something interesting. Here's a simple while loop:

```
i = 0
  while i < 5:
  print(i)
  i += 1
```

In this example, the while loop keeps running as long as the variable i is less than 5. The line i += 1 increases the value of i by 1 each time the loop runs. So, this loop prints the numbers 0, 1, 2, 3, and 4. Be careful with while loops. If the condition never becomes false, you'll create an infinite loop, which means the loop will keep running forever and can crash your program.

Combining if statements and loops can make your programs very powerful. Let's say you want to print only the even numbers from 0 to 10. You can use an if statement inside a for loop to do this:

```
for i in range(11):
  if i % 2 == 0:
  print(i)
```

The % symbol is the modulus operator, which gives the remainder of a division. If a number is even, the remainder when you divide it by 2 is 0. The if statement checks this condition, and if it's true, the number is printed.

Now, let's look at how you can use loops to work with lists. Imagine you have a list of your favorite animals and you want to print each one with a message. Here's how you can do it:

```python
animals = ["dog", "cat", "elephant"]
for animal in animals:
    print("I love", animal)
```

This for loop goes through each item in the list animals and prints a message for each one. You can also use the index of each item in the list with the enumerate function:

```python
animals = ["dog", "cat", "elephant"]
for index, animal in enumerate(animals):
    print(index, ":", animal)
```

The enumerate function adds a counter to the list, and the loop prints the index and the animal. This can be useful if you need to know the position of each item in the list.

Sometimes, you need to break out of a loop early. You can do this with the break statement. For example, let's say you're looking for a specific animal in a list and you want to stop searching once you find it:

```python
animals = ["dog", "cat", "elephant"]
for animal in animals:
    if animal == "cat":
        print("Found the cat!")
        break
    print("Looking at", animal)
```

In this example, the loop goes through each animal in the list. When it finds "cat," it prints a message and breaks out of the loop. The loop stops running, even if there are more items in the list.

There's also a continue statement that skips the rest of the code inside the loop for the current iteration and moves to the next iteration. Here's an example:

```
for i in range(10):
    if i % 2 == 0:
        continue
    print(i)
```

This loop prints only the odd numbers from 0 to 9. When the loop encounters an even number, the continue statement skips the rest of the code inside the loop and goes to the next iteration.

Another useful control structure is the nested loop. This is a loop inside another loop. You might use nested loops when you need to repeat a set of actions for each item in a list, and then repeat that whole process for another list. Here's an example:

```
for i in range(3):
    for j in range(2):
        print("i =", i, "j =", j)
```

In this example, the outer loop runs three times, and for each iteration of the outer loop, the inner loop runs twice. So, the print statement runs a total of six times. Nested loops can be very useful, but they can also make your code more complex, so use them carefully.

Let's switch gears and talk about another powerful feature of Python: list comprehensions. List comprehensions provide a concise way to create lists. They can replace a for loop that generates a list. Here's an example of a basic list comprehension:

```
squares = [i ** 2 for i in range(10)]
    print(squares)
```

This creates a list of the squares of numbers from 0 to 9. It's equivalent to writing a for loop that appends the squares to a list, but it's much shorter and easier to read. You can also include an if condition in a list comprehension:

```
even_squares = [i ** 2 for i in range(10) if i % 2 == 0]
  print(even_squares)
```

This creates a list of the squares of even numbers from 0 to 9. List comprehensions are a very powerful and concise way to generate lists.

Now, let's talk about how you can use loops and if statements together to solve more complex problems. For example, let's say you have a list of numbers and you want to create a new list that contains only the even numbers:

```
numbers = [1, 2, 3, 4, 5, 6, 7, 8, 9, 10]
  even_numbers = []
  for number in numbers:
  if number % 2 == 0:
  even_numbers.append(number)
```

In this example, the for loop goes through each number in the list numbers. The if statement checks if the number is even. If it is, the number is added to the list even_numbers. You can also use a list comprehension to do the same thing:

```
even_numbers = [number for number in numbers if number % 2 == 0]
```

Both methods achieve the same result, but the list comprehension is more concise.

Another useful feature in Python is the ability to iterate over multiple lists at the same time using the zip function. This can be helpful when you need to combine data from different sources. Here's an example:

```
names = ["Alice", "Bob", "Charlie"]
```

```
ages = [10, 12, 11]
for name, age in zip(names, ages):
    print(name, "is", age, "years old")
```

In this example, the zip function combines the names and ages lists, and the for loop iterates over the pairs, printing a message for each one.

Understanding control structures is crucial for programming because they allow you to create flexible and efficient code. With if statements, loops, and list comprehensions, you can handle a wide range of tasks and solve complex problems. These tools form the backbone of most programs, and mastering them will give you a solid foundation in Python programming. As you practice using these control structures, you'll become more confident and capable of writing your own programs.

Chapter 4: Functions and Modules

In this chapter, we'll explore the magic of functions and modules. These tools help you organize your code, making it easier to read, write, and reuse. Functions and modules are like the building blocks of your programs, allowing you to break down complex tasks into simpler, manageable pieces.

Let's start with functions. A function is a block of code that performs a specific task. You can think of it as a mini-program within your program. Once you define a function, you can use it anytime you need to perform that task, without having to write the same code over and over again. This makes your code more organized and saves you a lot of time.

To define a function in Python, you use the def keyword, followed by the function name and parentheses. Inside the parentheses, you can list any parameters the function needs. Parameters are like variables that you pass into the function. Here's a simple example:

```
def greet(name):
    print("Hello,", name)
```

In this example, greet is the name of the function, and name is the parameter. The function prints a greeting using the name you pass to it. To call the function and see it in action, you simply write the function name and provide a value for the parameter:

greet("Alice")

When you run this code, Python will print "Hello, Alice." Functions can take multiple parameters. Here's an example of a function that adds two numbers:

```
def add_numbers(a, b):
    return a + b
```

In this example, add_numbers is the name of the function, and a and b are the parameters. The function adds the two numbers and returns the result. To use the function, you call it with two numbers:

```
result = add_numbers(3, 5)
    print(result)
```

Python will print 8, which is the sum of 3 and 5. The return statement is used to send the result back to the part of the program that called the function. This allows you to use the result in other parts of your program.

Functions are incredibly useful because they let you reuse code. If you find yourself writing the same code multiple times, you can put it in a function and call the function whenever you need it. This not only saves time but also makes your code easier to read and maintain.

Now, let's talk about a special type of function called a lambda function. Lambda functions are small, anonymous functions defined with the lambda keyword. They are used for simple tasks that you only need to do once or twice. Here's an example of a lambda function that adds two numbers:

```
add = lambda a, b: a + b
```

This is equivalent to the add_numbers function we defined earlier, but it's written in a more compact form. You can call a lambda function in the same way you call a regular function:

```
result = add(3, 5)
  print(result)
```

Lambda functions are often used with other functions, such as map and filter, which apply a function to each item in a list. Here's an example of using a lambda function with map to double each number in a list:

```
numbers = [1, 2, 3, 4, 5]
  doubled = list(map(lambda x: x * 2, numbers))
  print(doubled)
```

The map function applies the lambda function to each item in the list numbers, doubling each one. The result is a new list with the doubled numbers.

Now that you understand functions, let's move on to modules. A module is a file that contains Python code. It can include functions, variables, and even other modules. Modules help you organize your code by grouping related functions and data together. This makes your code easier to manage and reuse.

Python comes with many built-in modules that provide useful functions and tools. You can also create your own modules or install third-party modules from the internet. To use a module, you need to import it into your program using the import statement. Here's an example of importing and using the math module, which provides mathematical functions and constants:

```
import math
  print(math.sqrt(16))
```

In this example, we import the math module and use its sqrt function to calculate the square root of 16. The import statement makes all the functions and variables in the module available to your program. You can use them by writing the module name followed by a dot and the function or variable name.

You can also import specific functions or variables from a module using the from ... import ... statement. Here's an example of importing just the sqrt function from the math module:

```
from math import sqrt
  print(sqrt(16))
```

This way, you can use the sqrt function directly without writing math. before it. If you want to give a function or variable a different name, you can use the as keyword:

```
from math import sqrt as square_root
  print(square_root(16))
```

This imports the sqrt function and gives it the name square_root in your program. Modules can make your code more organized and easier to read by keeping related functions and data together.

Let's create a simple module of our own. First, open a new file and write the following code:

```
def greet(name):
   print("Hello,", name)

def add_numbers(a, b):
   return a + b
```

Save the file with a name like mymodule.py. This file is now a module that you can import into your programs. To use it, create another Python file in the same directory and write:

```
import mymodule
  mymodule.greet("Alice")
  result = mymodule.add_numbers(3, 5)
  print(result)
```

When you run this code, Python will import the mymodule module and call its functions. This allows you to organize your code into separate files and reuse it across different programs.

Modules can also include variables and other data. Here's an example of a module with a variable and a function:

```
pi = 3.14159

def circumference(radius):
    return 2 * pi * radius
```

Save this code in a file named circle.py. To use it in your program, write:

```
import circle
  print(circle.pi)
  print(circle.circumference(5))
```

This imports the circle module and uses its variable and function. Modules make it easy to organize and reuse your code, especially for larger programs.

Python also has a feature called packages, which are collections of modules. A package is simply a directory that contains multiple modules. Each module is a file, and the package directory must include a special file named __init__.py, which can be empty or contain initialization code for the package.

Here's an example of creating a package. First, create a directory named mypackage. Inside this directory, create an empty file named __init__.py and a file named module1.py with the following code:

```
def greet(name):
    print("Hello,", name)
```

Next, create another file named module2.py with this code:

```
def add_numbers(a, b):
    return a + b
```

Now, you have a package with two modules. To use it in your program, write:

```
from mypackage import module1, module2
    module1.greet("Alice")
    result = module2.add_numbers(3, 5)
    print(result)
```

This imports the modules from the mypackage package and calls their functions. Packages allow you to organize your code into a hierarchy, making it easier to manage and navigate.

Understanding functions and modules is essential for writing clean, organized, and reusable code. Functions help you break down complex tasks into simpler pieces, while modules and packages help you group related functions and data together. As you write more programs, these tools will become invaluable for keeping your code manageable and efficient.

To recap, we've learned how to define and call functions, use lambda functions for simple tasks, and organize code with modules and packages. These concepts are the building blocks of effective programming and will help you write better code. As you practice using functions and modules, you'll become more confident and capable of tackling more complex projects.

Chapter 5: Working with Lists and Dictionaries

Lists and dictionaries are two super handy tools in Python that help you organize information. Think of them like containers where you can store different kinds of data. Let's explore how to use them and why they're so awesome.

Let's start with lists. A list is like a collection of items, such as a shopping list or a list of your favorite games. You create a list by putting items inside square brackets, separated by commas. For example, a list of numbers could look like this: [1, 2, 3, 4, 5]. You can put all sorts of things in a list, like numbers, words, or even other lists.

One cool thing about lists is that you can access each item by its position, called an index. In Python, the first item in a list is at position 0. So if you have a list called fruits with the items ["apple", "banana", "cherry"], fruits[0] gives you "apple."

You can also change items in a list. If you want to change "banana" to "blueberry" in the fruits list, you write fruits[1] = "blueberry." Lists are like playdough; you can reshape them whenever you need to.

Adding items to a list is easy with the append method. If you want to add

CHAPTER 5: WORKING WITH LISTS AND DICTIONARIES

"orange" to the fruits list, you write fruits.append("orange"). This sticks the new item at the end of the list. If you need to insert an item at a specific spot, use the insert method. For example, fruits.insert(1, "mango") adds "mango" at position 1, scooting everything else over to make room.

Sometimes you need to take items out of a list. The remove method does this. If you want to remove "cherry" from the fruits list, you write fruits.remove("cherry"). This takes out the first "cherry" it finds. If you don't know the item but know its position, use the pop method. For example, fruits.pop(2) removes the item at position 2.

Lists have lots of useful tricks. The sort method arranges the items in order. If you have a list of numbers, numbers.sort() will put them from smallest to biggest. The reverse method flips the list around. So, if you have a list like [1, 2, 3], numbers.reverse() changes it to [3, 2, 1].

Another neat thing you can do with lists is slicing. Slicing lets you grab a part of the list and make a new list from it. You use a colon to show the start and end positions. For example, if you have a list numbers = [0, 1, 2, 3, 4, 5], numbers[1:4] gives you a new list [1, 2, 3]. Slicing goes up to, but doesn't include, the end position.

Now that you've got a handle on lists, let's talk about dictionaries. A dictionary is like a real dictionary where you look up a word (the key) to find its definition (the value). In Python, dictionaries are made with curly braces. Each key-value pair is separated by a colon, and pairs are separated by commas. Here's an example: {"name": "Alice", "age": 10, "city": "Wonderland"}.

You get the values in a dictionary by their keys. If you have a dictionary called person, you get the name by writing person["name"], which would give you "Alice." Dictionaries are great for storing related information and finding it quickly.

Adding and updating values in a dictionary is simple. To add a new key-value pair, you write dictionary_name[key] = value. For example, to add a favorite color to the person dictionary, you write person["favorite_color"] = "blue." If the key already exists, this changes the value.

Taking items out of a dictionary can be done with the pop method or the del keyword. If you want to remove the age key from the person dictionary, you write person.pop("age") or del person["age"]. This takes out the key and its value.

Dictionaries have many useful methods too. The keys method returns all the keys in the dictionary, while the values method returns all the values. The items method gives you both keys and values. For example, person.keys() gives you ["name", "city", "favorite_color"].

You can loop through dictionaries just like lists. If you want to print all the keys and values in the person dictionary, you can use a for loop:

for key, value in person.items():
    print(key, ":", value)

This goes through each key-value pair and prints them. It's a handy way to see everything in your dictionary.

Lists and dictionaries are like the superheroes of data storage in Python. They make it easy to organize, access, and modify your data. Whether you're keeping track of scores in a game, storing information about your favorite characters, or just organizing your thoughts, lists and dictionaries are the tools you'll use.

Understanding how to work with lists and dictionaries is a big step in becoming a Python pro. They help you keep your data organized and make your code more efficient. As you practice using them, you'll discover all sorts of new ways to make your programs smarter and more fun to use. Keep exploring and experimenting, and you'll see how powerful these tools can be.

Chapter 6: Introduction to Object-Oriented Programming

Object-oriented programming, or OOP for short, is a way of thinking about and organizing your code that makes it easier to manage and use. OOP is all about creating objects, which are like little bundles of data and functions that work together. Let's dive into how OOP works in Python and why it's so useful.

An object is a collection of data (called attributes) and functions (called methods) that are grouped together. For example, think of a car. A car has attributes like color, brand, and speed. It also has methods like drive, stop, and honk. In OOP, you create a blueprint for an object called a class, and then you can make as many objects as you want from that blueprint. The class defines what attributes and methods the objects will have.

To define a class in Python, you use the class keyword followed by the class name. Here's a simple example of a class that represents a car:

```
class Car:
    def __init__(self, color, brand):
        self.color = color
        self.brand = brand

    def drive(self):
```

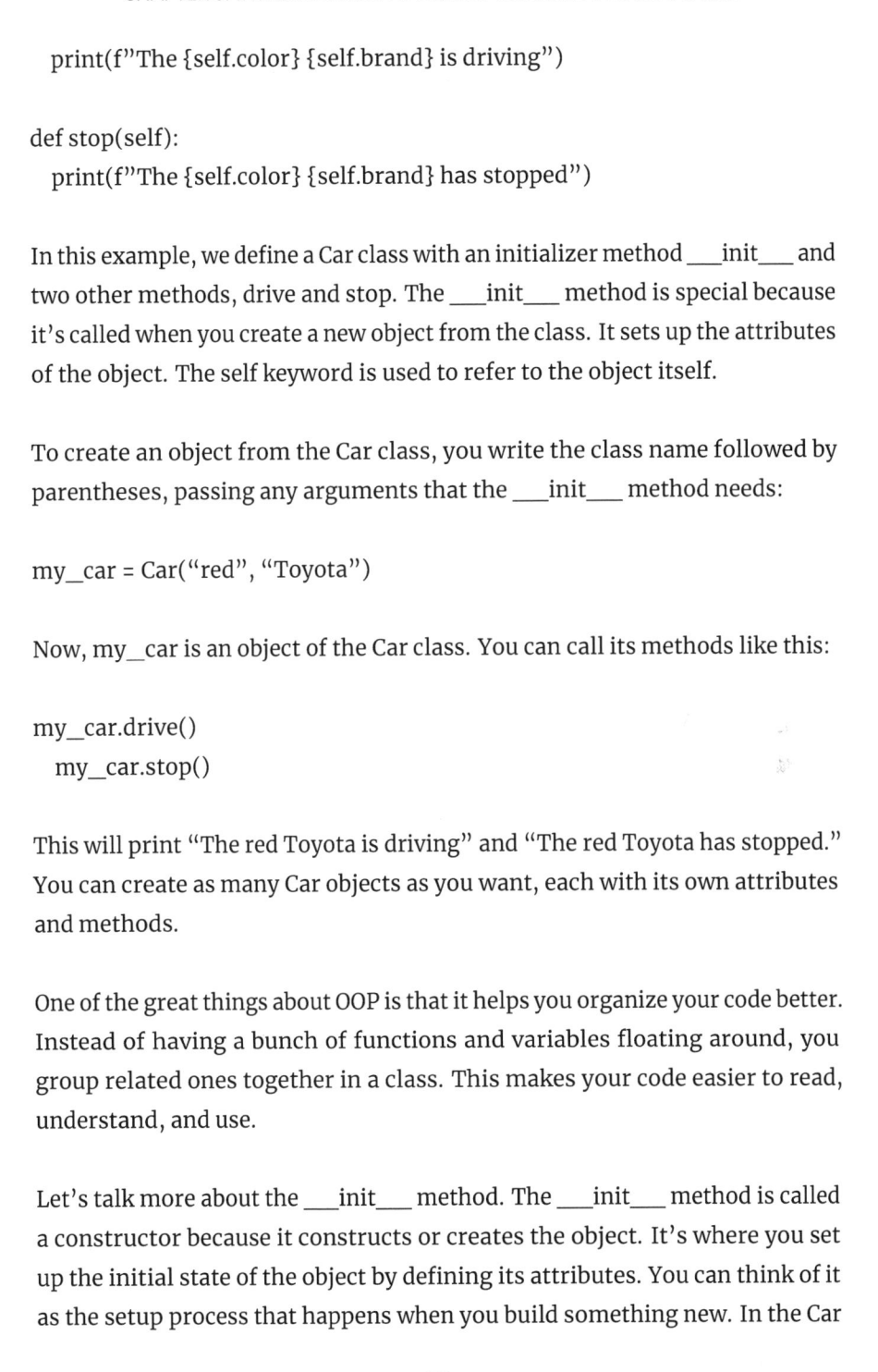

```
print(f"The {self.color} {self.brand} is driving")

def stop(self):
    print(f"The {self.color} {self.brand} has stopped")
```

In this example, we define a Car class with an initializer method __init__ and two other methods, drive and stop. The __init__ method is special because it's called when you create a new object from the class. It sets up the attributes of the object. The self keyword is used to refer to the object itself.

To create an object from the Car class, you write the class name followed by parentheses, passing any arguments that the __init__ method needs:

```
my_car = Car("red", "Toyota")
```

Now, my_car is an object of the Car class. You can call its methods like this:

```
my_car.drive()
  my_car.stop()
```

This will print "The red Toyota is driving" and "The red Toyota has stopped." You can create as many Car objects as you want, each with its own attributes and methods.

One of the great things about OOP is that it helps you organize your code better. Instead of having a bunch of functions and variables floating around, you group related ones together in a class. This makes your code easier to read, understand, and use.

Let's talk more about the __init__ method. The __init__ method is called a constructor because it constructs or creates the object. It's where you set up the initial state of the object by defining its attributes. You can think of it as the setup process that happens when you build something new. In the Car class, the __init__ method takes two parameters, color and brand, and sets the corresponding attributes.

Methods are like the actions that an object can perform. In the Car class, drive and stop are methods. You define methods inside the class, and they always take self as the first parameter. This is how they can access the object's attributes and other methods. When you call a method on an object, Python automatically passes the object as the first argument.

Now, let's explore another important concept in OOP called inheritance. Inheritance allows you to create a new class that is based on an existing class. The new class, called a subclass, inherits all the attributes and methods of the existing class, called a superclass. This is useful because it lets you reuse code and build on what you've already done.

Here's an example of inheritance. Let's say we want to create a subclass of Car called ElectricCar that adds some new attributes and methods:

```
class ElectricCar(Car):
    def __init__(self, color, brand, battery_size):
    super().__init__(color, brand)
    self.battery_size = battery_size

def charge(self):
    print(f"The {self.color} {self.brand} is charging with a {self.battery_size}kWh battery")
```

In this example, ElectricCar is a subclass of Car. It inherits the attributes and methods of the Car class, but it also adds a new attribute called battery_size and a new method called charge. The super() function is used to call the __init__ method of the superclass, so we don't have to rewrite that part.

You can create an ElectricCar object just like you would a Car object:

```
my_electric_car = ElectricCar("blue", "Tesla", 75)
  my_electric_car.drive()
  my_electric_car.charge()
```

This will print "The blue Tesla is driving" and "The blue Tesla is charging with a 75kWh battery." Inheritance is a powerful way to extend the functionality of your classes and keep your code organized.

Another important concept in OOP is encapsulation. Encapsulation means keeping the details of how something works hidden away, so you only need to know how to use it, not how it works inside. In Python, you can make an attribute private by starting its name with an underscore. This tells other programmers that the attribute is not meant to be accessed directly.

Here's an example of encapsulation in the Car class:

```
class Car:
    def __init__(self, color, brand):
    self._color = color
    self._brand = brand

def drive(self):
    print(f"The {self._color} {self._brand} is driving")

def stop(self):
    print(f"The {self._color} {self._brand} has stopped")

def set_color(self, color):
    self._color = color

def get_color(self):
    return self._color
```

In this example, the attributes _color and _brand are private. We also added methods set_color and get_color to change and access the color attribute. This way, you control how the attributes are used and changed, which helps prevent mistakes and keeps your code cleaner.

Encapsulation makes your code safer and easier to use. When you hide the details of how something works, you can change the implementation without affecting other parts of your program. This is like using a remote control for a toy car. You don't need to know how the electronics inside work; you just need to know which buttons to press.

Polymorphism is another key concept in OOP. Polymorphism means "many forms," and it allows you to use the same method name in different classes. Each class can provide its own implementation of the method. This makes your code more flexible and easier to extend.

Here's an example of polymorphism with the Car and ElectricCar classes:

```
class Car:
    def drive(self):
    print("The car is driving")

class ElectricCar(Car):
    def drive(self):
    print("The electric car is driving silently")
```

In this example, both Car and ElectricCar have a drive method, but they do different things. When you call the drive method on a Car object, you get one result, and when you call it on an ElectricCar object, you get a different result.

Polymorphism is useful because it allows you to write code that works with objects of different classes. For example, you can create a function that takes a Car object and calls its drive method, and it will work with any subclass of

Car:

```
def start_driving(car):
    car.drive()

my_car = Car()
    my_electric_car = ElectricCar()

start_driving(my_car)
    start_driving(my_electric_car)
```

This function calls the drive method on whatever object you pass to it. If you pass a Car object, it drives like a regular car. If you pass an ElectricCar object, it drives silently. Polymorphism makes your code more flexible and easier to extend.

OOP helps you think about and organize your code in a more logical way. It allows you to create complex programs by combining simpler pieces, each with its own responsibilities. This way, you can build and maintain larger and more complex software without getting lost in a maze of code.

As you continue learning about Python and writing your own programs, you'll see how OOP makes your life easier. By using classes, objects, inheritance, encapsulation, and polymorphism, you can create more powerful and flexible programs. These concepts might seem a bit tricky at first, but with practice, you'll start to see how they fit together and make your code better.

Chapter 7: Working with Files

Working with files is an important skill in programming because it allows you to read from and write to external data sources. This means you can save information, load data from a file, and even process large amounts of data easily. Understanding how to handle files in Python opens up many possibilities for creating useful and interactive programs.

First, let's talk about reading from a file. Reading from a file means opening a file and extracting its contents so you can use that information in your program. Python makes this process straightforward with the open function. The open function requires the name of the file you want to read and the mode in which you want to open the file. To read a file, you use the mode "r," which stands for read. Here's how you do it:

file = open("example.txt", "r")

This line of code opens a file named example.txt in read mode. Once the file is open, you can read its contents using various methods. The read method reads the entire file and returns its contents as a single string:

contents = file.read()
　　print(contents)

After reading the file, it's important to close it to free up system resources:

file.close()

While this method works, there's an even better way to handle files in Python using the with statement. The with statement automatically closes the file for you, even if an error occurs. Here's how you do it:

```
with open("example.txt", "r") as file:
    contents = file.read()
    print(contents)
```

This approach is cleaner and safer. The with statement ensures that the file is properly closed after you're done working with it.

Sometimes, you might want to read a file line by line instead of reading the entire file at once. This is useful when dealing with large files. You can use the readline method to read one line at a time:

```
with open("example.txt", "r") as file:
    line = file.readline()
    while line:
        print(line, end="")
        line = file.readline()
```

The end="" part ensures that Python doesn't add an extra newline character after each line. This method reads and prints each line in the file until there are no more lines to read.

You can also read all the lines of a file into a list using the readlines method:

```
with open("example.txt", "r") as file:
    lines = file.readlines()
    for line in lines:
        print(line, end="")
```

This method reads all the lines of the file and stores them in a list called lines. You can then loop through the list and print each line.

Now, let's talk about writing to a file. Writing to a file means opening a file and adding or updating its contents. You use the open function with the mode "w" for write or "a" for append. The write mode creates a new file or overwrites an existing file, while the append mode adds new data to the end of an existing file.

Here's how you write to a file in write mode:

```
with open("output.txt", "w") as file:
    file.write("Hello, world!\n")
    file.write("This is a new line of text.\n")
```

This code creates a file named output.txt and writes two lines of text to it. If the file already exists, it will be overwritten. To add data to an existing file without overwriting it, use the append mode:

```
with open("output.txt", "a") as file:
    file.write("Appending a new line of text.\n")
```

This code opens the file in append mode and adds a new line of text to the end of the file.

Reading from and writing to files is great for working with text data, but sometimes you need to work with more structured data, like CSV files. CSV stands for Comma-Separated Values, and it's a common format for storing tabular data. Each line in a CSV file represents a row of data, with values separated by commas.

Python's csv module makes it easy to read from and write to CSV files. Here's how you read a CSV file:

```
import csv

with open("data.csv", "r") as file:
    reader = csv.reader(file)
    for row in reader:
        print(row)
```

This code opens a file named data.csv and uses the csv.reader function to read its contents. The reader object iterates over each row in the file, and you can print or process each row as needed.

To write to a CSV file, use the csv.writer function:

```
import csv

with open("output.csv", "w", newline="") as file:
    writer = csv.writer(file)
    writer.writerow(["Name", "Age", "City"])
    writer.writerow(["Alice", 10, "Wonderland"])
    writer.writerow(["Bob", 12, "Builderland"])
```

This code creates a file named output.csv and writes three rows of data to it. The newline="" argument ensures that Python doesn't add extra newline characters between rows.

Working with files also means handling errors gracefully. Sometimes, things go wrong when reading or writing files, such as the file not existing or permission issues. Python provides a way to handle these errors using try and except blocks. Here's an example:

```
try:
    with open("nonexistent_file.txt", "r") as file:
        contents = file.read()
```

```
    print(contents)
except FileNotFoundError:
    print("The file does not exist.")
```

This code tries to open a file that doesn't exist. When it fails, Python raises a FileNotFoundError, which is caught by the except block. This prevents your program from crashing and allows you to handle the error gracefully.

Files can also store more complex data structures, like dictionaries and lists. Python's json module makes it easy to read and write JSON (JavaScript Object Notation) data, which is a popular format for exchanging data between programs. Here's how you write a dictionary to a JSON file:

```
import json

data = {
    "name": "Alice",
    "age": 10,
    "city": "Wonderland"
}

with open("data.json", "w") as file:
    json.dump(data, file)
```

This code creates a file named data.json and writes the data dictionary to it in JSON format. To read the JSON data back into a dictionary, use the json.load function:

```
import json

with open("data.json", "r") as file:
    data = json.load(file)
    print(data)
```

This code opens the data.json file, reads its contents, and converts the JSON data back into a Python dictionary.

Another useful file format is the pickle format, which allows you to serialize and deserialize Python objects. Serialization means converting an object into a format that can be easily stored and transmitted, while deserialization is the reverse process. Here's how you serialize an object to a file using the pickle module:

```
import pickle

data = {
    "name": "Alice",
    "age": 10,
    "city": "Wonderland"
}

with open("data.pkl", "wb") as file:
    pickle.dump(data, file)
```

This code creates a file named data.pkl and writes the data dictionary to it in pickle format. The wb mode stands for write binary, which is needed for binary file formats like pickle. To read the data back into a dictionary, use the pickle.load function:

```
import pickle

with open("data.pkl", "rb") as file:
    data = pickle.load(file)
    print(data)
```

This code opens the data.pkl file, reads its contents, and converts the pickle data back into a Python dictionary. The rb mode stands for read binary, which is needed for reading binary files.

Understanding how to work with files is a fundamental skill in programming. It allows you to save and load data, process large amounts of information, and exchange data with other programs. Whether you're working with simple text files, structured CSV files, or complex data formats like JSON and pickle, Python provides the tools you need to handle files efficiently and effectively.

By mastering file handling in Python, you can create more powerful and versatile programs that can interact with the world outside your code. As you practice reading from and writing to files, you'll become more confident in your ability to manage data and create programs that can store and retrieve information seamlessly.

Chapter 8: Fun with Turtle Graphics

Turtle Graphics is a fun and interactive way to create drawings and shapes using Python. It's like having a little turtle that follows your instructions to draw pictures on the screen. Turtle Graphics is great for kids because it combines creativity with programming skills, making learning both enjoyable and educational.

To start using Turtle Graphics, you need to import the turtle module. The turtle module provides all the tools you need to control the turtle and create your drawings. Once you have imported the module, you can create a turtle object that will act as your drawing tool.

The turtle starts in the center of the screen, facing right. You can move the turtle forward, backward, left, or right, and it will draw lines as it moves. Let's begin by making the turtle draw a simple shape, like a square.

The main commands to move the turtle are forward() and right(). The forward() command makes the turtle move straight ahead by a specified number of steps, while the right() command makes the turtle turn right by a specified number of degrees.

For example, to draw a square, you can move the turtle forward and then turn it right by 90 degrees, repeating this process four times. This will make the turtle draw four sides, forming a square.

Now, let's explore some more advanced movements and see how to draw different shapes and patterns. You can use the left() command to turn the turtle left by a specified number of degrees. This is useful for creating more complex shapes, like stars and polygons.

One fun shape to draw is a star. To draw a star, you need to use both the forward() and left() commands in a loop. Each point of the star requires the turtle to move forward and then turn left by a specific angle. The turtle will keep drawing until all the points of the star are completed.

Besides moving the turtle around, you can also control its appearance. You can change the turtle's color, shape, and size using various commands. For instance, you can use the color() command to change the color of the turtle's pen, making your drawings more colorful and interesting.

If you want to create more complex drawings, you can use loops to repeat commands. Loops are powerful tools that let you execute a block of code multiple times, which is perfect for drawing patterns. For example, you can use a for loop to draw a spiral. By gradually increasing the distance the turtle moves forward with each iteration, you can create a spiral effect.

Turtle Graphics also allows you to fill shapes with color. You can use the begin_fill() and end_fill() commands to start and stop filling a shape. Any shape drawn between these two commands will be filled with the current pen color.

Another exciting feature of Turtle Graphics is its ability to respond to user input. You can make your turtle drawing interactive by capturing keyboard and mouse events. For example, you can write a program that lets you control the turtle using the arrow keys on your keyboard. This makes drawing even more fun, as you can guide the turtle around the screen in real-time.

When working with Turtle Graphics, you might want to clear the screen and start over without closing the program. You can use the clear() command to erase all the drawings on the screen while keeping the turtle in its current position. This is handy when you're experimenting with different shapes and patterns and want to start fresh.

Sometimes, you might want to hide the turtle while it's drawing to get a better view of the drawing process. You can use the hideturtle() command to hide the turtle and the showturtle() command to make it visible again. This helps you focus on the drawing itself rather than the turtle's movements.

In addition to basic shapes and patterns, you can also create more intricate designs by combining multiple shapes. For instance, you can draw a flower by arranging several circles in a circular pattern. By adjusting the size and position of each circle, you can create beautiful and complex designs.

Another fun project with Turtle Graphics is drawing a maze. You can create a simple maze by drawing a series of connected lines and then challenge yourself or your friends to navigate the turtle through the maze. This project combines creativity with problem-solving skills, making it an enjoyable and educational activity.

Turtle Graphics is also a great way to learn about coordinates and geometry. Each point on the turtle's screen has an (x, y) coordinate, with (0, 0) being the center of the screen. You can move the turtle to specific coordinates using the goto() command. This helps you understand how shapes are positioned on the screen and how coordinates work.

You can even animate your turtle drawings by introducing delays between commands. By adding a small delay between each movement, you can create animations that show the drawing process step by step. This makes your drawings come to life and adds an extra layer of fun to your projects.

As you become more comfortable with Turtle Graphics, you can start experimenting with creating your own designs and patterns. The possibilities are endless, and you can let your imagination run wild. Whether you're drawing simple shapes or complex patterns, Turtle Graphics is a fantastic way to practice your programming skills while having fun.

Turtle Graphics is a wonderful tool for young programmers. It combines the joy of drawing with the excitement of coding, making learning an enjoyable experience. By working with Turtle Graphics, you can develop a better understanding of programming concepts, improve your problem-solving skills, and unleash your creativity. Keep exploring, experimenting, and creating, and you'll discover the endless possibilities that Turtle Graphics has to offer.

Chapter 9: Simple Game Development

Creating your own games is one of the most fun and rewarding things you can do with programming. Games are not only entertaining to play, but they also help you learn important coding concepts. In this chapter, we'll dive into simple game development using Python. You'll learn how to create interactive games, control game characters, and handle user input. Let's get started with the basics of making a simple game.

The first thing you need to do when creating a game is to set up the game window. This is the screen where all the action happens. We'll use a library called Pygame, which makes it easy to create games in Python. You need to install Pygame before using it. You can do this by typing pip install pygame in your terminal or command prompt.

Once Pygame is installed, you can start by creating the game window. You do this by initializing Pygame and setting the size of the window. Here's a bit of code to create a game window:

```
import pygame

pygame.init()
    screen = pygame.display.set_mode((800, 600))
    pygame.display.set_caption("Simple Game")
```

The code initializes Pygame, sets the window size to 800 by 600 pixels, and gives the window a title. Now, you have a blank canvas where you can draw and animate your game.

Next, you need to create a game loop. The game loop is the heart of any game. It runs continuously, updating the game state and drawing everything on the screen. The game loop keeps the game running and responding to user input. Here's how you set up a basic game loop:

```
running = True
    while running:
    for event in pygame.event.get():
    if event.type == pygame.QUIT:
    running = False

screen.fill((0, 0, 0))
    pygame.display.update()

pygame.quit()
```

In this code, the game loop runs as long as the variable running is True. Inside the loop, you check for events like quitting the game. If the user closes the window, the game loop stops. The screen.fill((0, 0, 0)) line fills the screen with a black color, and pygame.display.update() updates the display with the new frame. Finally, pygame.quit() cleans up when the game is over.

Now that you have a basic game loop, let's add a game character. A game character is usually represented by an image called a sprite. You can load an image and draw it on the screen using Pygame. Here's how you can do it:

```
player = pygame.image.load("player.png")
    player_x = 370
    player_y = 480
```

```
screen.blit(player, (player_x, player_y))
pygame.display.update()
```

In this example, you load an image called player.png and set its initial position on the screen using player_x and player_y. The screen.blit() function draws the image at the specified position. The pygame.display.update() function refreshes the screen to show the new frame.

To make your game character move, you need to handle user input. The user can control the game character using the keyboard or mouse. Here's how you can move the character left and right using the arrow keys:

```
player_x_change = 0

for event in pygame.event.get():
    if event.type == pygame.KEYDOWN:
    if event.key == pygame.K_LEFT:
    player_x_change = -0.3
    if event.key == pygame.K_RIGHT:
    player_x_change = 0.3
    if event.type == pygame.KEYUP:
    if event.key == pygame.K_LEFT or event.key == pygame.K_RIGHT:
    player_x_change = 0

player_x += player_x_change
```

In this code, you check for KEYDOWN and KEYUP events. When the left arrow key is pressed, player_x_change is set to -0.3 to move the character to the left. When the right arrow key is pressed, player_x_change is set to 0.3 to move the character to the right. When the keys are released, player_x_change is set to 0 to stop the movement. The player_x += player_x_change line updates the character's position based on the change in x.

You can also add boundaries to make sure the character doesn't move off the screen. Here's how you can do it:

```
if player_x <= 0:
    player_x = 0
elif player_x >= 736:
    player_x = 736
```

This code checks if the character's x position is less than or equal to 0 or greater than or equal to 736 (the screen width minus the character's width). If it is, the position is reset to keep the character within the screen boundaries.

Next, let's add some game elements like enemies. Enemies can move around the screen and interact with the game character. Here's how you can create an enemy:

```
enemy = pygame.image.load("enemy.png")
    enemy_x = random.randint(0, 736)
    enemy_y = random.randint(50, 150)
    enemy_x_change = 0.3

screen.blit(enemy, (enemy_x, enemy_y))
```

In this example, you load an image called enemy.png and set its initial position randomly within a specified range. The enemy_x_change variable controls the speed and direction of the enemy's movement.

To make the enemy move, you can update its position in the game loop:

```
enemy_x += enemy_x_change

if enemy_x <= 0:
    enemy_x_change = 0.3
```

```
enemy_y += enemy_y_change
elif enemy_x >= 736:
enemy_x_change = -0.3
enemy_y += enemy_y_change
```

This code moves the enemy horizontally across the screen. When the enemy reaches the edge of the screen, it changes direction and moves down. You can adjust the speed and movement pattern to make the game more challenging.

Collisions are an important part of any game. You need to check if the game character collides with an enemy or any other game element. Pygame provides a simple way to check for collisions using rectangles. You can create rectangles around the game character and the enemy and check if they overlap:

```
def is_collision(player_x, player_y, enemy_x, enemy_y):
    distance = math.sqrt((math.pow(player_x - enemy_x, 2)) + (math.pow(player_y - enemy_y, 2)))
    if distance < 27:
    return True
    else:
    return False

collision = is_collision(player_x, player_y, enemy_x, enemy_y)
    if collision:
    print("Collision detected!")
```

In this example, the is_collision function calculates the distance between the game character and the enemy using the Pythagorean theorem. If the distance is less than a certain threshold, it means a collision has occurred. You can then handle the collision by ending the game or taking other actions.

Another important aspect of game development is keeping track of the score. You can display the score on the screen using Pygame's font module. Here's how you can create and update the score:

```
score_value = 0
    font = pygame.font.Font('freesansbold.ttf', 32)
    text_x = 10
    text_y = 10

def show_score(x, y):
    score = font.render("Score: " + str(score_value), True, (255, 255, 255))
    screen.blit(score, (x, y))
```

In this code, you create a font object and set the position for the score display. The show_score function renders the score text and draws it on the screen. You can call this function in the game loop to update the score continuously.

Finally, adding sound effects and music can make your game more engaging. Pygame allows you to load and play sound files. Here's how you can add sound effects:

```
sound = pygame.mixer.Sound("explosion.wav")
    sound.play()
```

This code loads a sound file called explosion.wav and plays it. You can play sound effects when certain events occur, like when the game character collides with an enemy or scores a point.

Creating a simple game involves combining all these elements: setting up the game window, creating a game loop, handling user input, moving game characters, checking for collisions, updating the score, and adding sound effects. As you gain experience, you can create more complex games with multiple levels, different types of enemies, and advanced graphics.

Game development is a great way to practice your programming skills and bring your ideas to life. By understanding the basics of Pygame and how to create a simple game, you're on your way to making your own interactive and entertaining projects. Keep experimenting, adding new features, and challenging yourself to create more advanced games.

Chapter 10: Building Your First Project

Creating your own projects can be one of the most exciting parts of learning to program. This is where you get to apply everything you've learned to make something cool and unique. Let's build a simple project that combines many of the concepts we've covered so far. We'll make a basic calculator that can do addition, subtraction, multiplication, and division. This calculator will have a user-friendly interface where you can input numbers and select operations.

To build our calculator, we'll use a library called Tkinter. Tkinter helps you create graphical user interfaces (GUIs) so you can interact with your program in a more visual way. It's like turning your Python script into an app with buttons and text fields.

First, we need to set up the environment and create the main window for our calculator. The main window is where everything will be displayed, like the buttons and the screen for showing the numbers and results. We'll use Tkinter to set up this window.

Once we have the main window, we can add a text field at the top where the numbers and results will be displayed. This text field will act like the screen on a real calculator. You type in numbers, and it shows you what you typed and the results of your calculations.

Next, we need to create buttons for the numbers 0 through 9. These buttons

CHAPTER 10: BUILDING YOUR FIRST PROJECT

will allow you to input numbers into the calculator. When you click a number button, the number will appear in the text field. This is where we'll use some simple functions to handle button clicks and update the text field.

We'll also need buttons for the arithmetic operations: addition, subtraction, multiplication, and division. When you click one of these buttons, the calculator will store the current number and the operation you want to perform. Then, when you input the next number and hit the equals button, the calculator will perform the operation and display the result.

To make sure our calculator works smoothly, we need to handle a few more details. For example, we should ensure the calculator doesn't try to divide by zero, as this would cause an error. We'll also want to add a clear button to reset the text field and start a new calculation.

Here's a simplified overview of how the calculator works:

1. Set up the main window using Tkinter.
    2. Add a text field for displaying numbers and results.
    3. Create buttons for numbers and place them on the window.
    4. Create buttons for operations and place them on the window.
    5. Write functions to handle button clicks and update the text field.
    6. Write functions to perform calculations and display the results.

The main window is like the frame of your calculator. Think of it as a blank canvas where you'll place all the buttons and the screen. Tkinter makes it easy to create this window and set its size and title.

The text field acts as the display screen of the calculator. It shows what numbers you've entered and the results of your calculations. This is where you see everything happening in real-time.

The number buttons let you input numbers into the calculator. Each button represents a digit from 0 to 9. When you press a button, the corresponding number appears on the screen. This makes it easy to enter numbers and perform calculations.

The operation buttons let you choose what kind of calculation you want to do. For example, you can add, subtract, multiply, or divide numbers. When you press an operation button, the calculator stores the current number and waits for you to enter the next number.

To make sure everything works together smoothly, we need some functions to handle the button clicks and perform the calculations. These functions are like the brain of the calculator. They take care of storing numbers, performing operations, and updating the display screen.

One important thing to handle is user input. For example, when you press a number button, the calculator should add that number to the current input. When you press an operation button, it should store the current number and operation, then clear the input for the next number.

Another important function is the equals button. This button performs the calculation based on the stored number and operation, then displays the result. It's like hitting the equals sign on a real calculator to see the final answer.

We also need to make sure the calculator can handle errors gracefully. For example, if you try to divide by zero, the calculator should display an error message instead of crashing. This makes your calculator more robust and user-friendly.

Finally, adding a clear button allows you to reset the calculator and start a new calculation. This is useful if you make a mistake or want to perform a new calculation without closing the program.

Building a project like this helps you see how different programming concepts come together to create something useful and fun. You get to practice working with libraries, handling user input, and making your program interact with users in a real-world way.

By understanding these concepts and how they fit together, you can create your own projects and bring your ideas to life. This is what makes programming so exciting and rewarding – the ability to create, experiment, and see your creations come to life on the screen.

Conclusion

Congratulations on reaching the end of this book! By now, you've learned so much about Python programming, from basic concepts to building your own projects. Let's take a moment to reflect on everything you've accomplished and see how all the pieces fit together.

We started our journey by understanding what Python is and why it's such a great language for beginners. Python's simplicity and readability make it easy to learn and use, which is why it's perfect for kids like you who are just getting started with programming. We also set up Python on your computer and wrote your first program – the classic "Hello, world!" This was the first step into the fascinating world of coding.

Next, we dove into basic Python concepts. We talked about variables, which are like little containers that store information. You learned how to create variables to hold different types of data, such as numbers, strings, and floats. We also explored basic arithmetic operations and saw how Python can help you do math. You discovered how to use comments to make your code more understandable and how important it is to keep your code organized and readable.

We then moved on to control structures, which are the building blocks of any program. You learned about if statements, which let you make decisions in your code based on certain conditions. This is like asking questions and doing

CONCLUSION

something based on the answers. You also learned about loops, which let you repeat actions multiple times without having to write the same code over and over. We looked at for loops and while loops, which are powerful tools for automating repetitive tasks.

Functions and modules were our next big topic. Functions are like little helpers that perform specific tasks for you. You learned how to define functions and call them whenever you need them. This helps you keep your code organized and reusable. We also talked about modules, which are collections of functions and tools that you can use in your programs. Python comes with many built-in modules that make your life easier, and you also learned how to create your own modules.

Lists and dictionaries were up next. Lists are like collections of items that you can store and manage in one place. You learned how to create lists, add and remove items, and access items by their position. We also explored slicing, which lets you take parts of a list to create a new list. Dictionaries are similar to lists but store data as key-value pairs. This makes them perfect for storing related information and accessing it quickly. You learned how to create dictionaries, add and remove items, and loop through them to access the data.

Object-oriented programming, or OOP, was a big milestone in our journey. OOP helps you think about and organize your code in a more logical way by grouping related data and functions into objects. You learned about classes and objects, which are the building blocks of OOP. We talked about inheritance, which lets you create new classes based on existing ones, and polymorphism, which lets you use the same method names in different classes. Encapsulation was another key concept, helping you keep the details of how something works hidden away, so you only need to know how to use it.

Working with files was our next topic. You discovered how to read from and write to files, which is important for storing and retrieving data. We looked at different file formats, such as text files and CSV files, and saw how Python makes it easy to work with them. You learned about the json and pickle modules, which let you store more complex data structures like dictionaries and lists. Handling errors gracefully using try and except blocks was another important skill you picked up, making your programs more robust and user-friendly.

Turtle Graphics brought some fun into our programming journey. You learned how to create drawings and shapes using Python's turtle module. This is like having a little turtle that follows your instructions to draw pictures on the screen. You discovered how to move the turtle, change its appearance, and create complex shapes and patterns. Turtle Graphics is a great way to practice programming while unleashing your creativity.

Simple game development was another exciting chapter. We used the Pygame library to create a basic game. You learned how to set up the game window, create a game loop, and handle user input. We added game characters, made them move, and checked for collisions. You also discovered how to keep track of the score and add sound effects to make the game more engaging. Game development combines many programming concepts and is a great way to see your code come to life.

Finally, we built a complete project from scratch. This project combined everything you've learned into a single program. You planned the project, set up the environment, and created the main window using Tkinter. You added buttons and text fields, handled user input, and performed calculations. This project showed you how to bring all the pieces together to create something functional and useful.

Throughout this journey, you've learned not just how to write code but also how to think like a programmer. You've developed problem-solving skills, learned to break down complex tasks into smaller, manageable pieces, and discovered the importance of organizing your code. You've seen how powerful and flexible Python is and how you can use it to create all sorts of programs, from simple scripts to complex games.

Learning to program is like learning a new language. The more you practice, the better you get. By building projects, experimenting with new ideas, and exploring different concepts, you'll continue to improve your skills and become a more confident programmer. Remember, every great programmer started where you are now, with curiosity and a desire to learn.

As you continue your programming journey, keep challenging yourself with new projects and ideas. Try building a game, creating a drawing, or solving a problem that interests you. Use the skills you've learned to explore new libraries and tools, and don't be afraid to make mistakes. Every mistake is an opportunity to learn something new and become a better programmer.

Python is a fantastic language to start with because it's both powerful and easy to learn. It's used by beginners and professionals alike, and it's the language of choice for many fields, from web development to data science. By mastering Python, you've opened up a world of possibilities. Whether you want to build websites, analyze data, create games, or even explore artificial intelligence, Python has the tools and libraries to help you achieve your goals.

Programming is a journey, and you've made an incredible start. Keep coding, keep learning, and most importantly, keep having fun. The world of programming is full of exciting opportunities and endless possibilities. With the skills you've gained, you're ready to explore and create amazing things. Happy coding!

Made in the USA
Columbia, SC
11 March 2025